OLD MONARCH

OLD MONARCH

Poems

Courtney Marie Andrews

Andrews McMeel
PUBLISHING®

For those brave enough to:
see, transform, become.

SONORAN
MILKWEED

BORN

So, this is the end.

More of a window,
less of a hallway

where we sit still,
wait and witness,
our long years

as all who follow
reenact our mistakes,
a perennial happening.

Some will stumble up
the staircase; others
never find the door.

THE SUN NEVER DESPAIRS

Today the sun mocks my despair.

"Get out of bed!" he says.
"I do, without hesitation.

Look outside!
I look every morning with joy.

Be grateful!
Each night I thank the moon for letting me rest."

Oh, sun, why must you make it seem so easy?
I close the curtains, only to fall back asleep.

A CHILD'S PROMISE

Some days I miss the vastness of the Sonoran sky.
Lavender in the crib of dusk, rocking Arizona to rest,
looping highways of inconceivable futures,

smells of wet cholla and mother chain-smoking Camels,
eyes glued to channel 10 as I climbed our local willow,
screaming, "Mom, look! The sunset!"

Often, I would fantasize about an imaginary portal—a world
beyond a dirt pit. She brushed off my plead, avoiding the colors
of dull days turning over.

Eventually, as a means of protection, I made a child's promise:
if I ever saw something beautiful, I must announce,
"I *see* you."

BEFORE IT ALL

Before it all,
back when I was still mystified
by earth's daily treasures
—with the confidence of a naive mare,
I charged through the garden, crushing
dandelions on my path.
Eyes toward the stars, yearning
for what lay beyond the fence.
I misunderstood in my youth
that every flower needs tended to.
Even life's smallest wonders
come with consequence.

Your mother's horse, Freedom,
broke the garden fence over and over
as your frustrated father
stood at the scene,
fat moon heavy in the night,
cursing his godless sky
like a priest without religion.
Still, time after time, he rebuilt it.

As I look back on our adolescence,
what comes to mind,
not the sweet kisses in the snow
or the late-night communions on Asher's porch
but the horse taking the garden for granted
—too occupied with possibility.
I broke free, time after time,
and you always rebuilt the fence.
Before it all, *you loved me.*

CALCULATED MAGIC

You are my illusion, water in the desert,
a mirage—master of magic tricks.
I am your rotten prickly pear, sweet
up until the end. Even when I disappear
from your night, you come conjuring me
back with words of voracity, when I am
lucid as waving agave. I believe
every charming word you say.

GRATITUDE FOR BLUE

Hallelujah for the Montana sky,
lakes, ponds, lazy long rivers,
Frank Sinatra's eyes, railroad
overalls—at times, my disposition.

We are so lucky to see a pigment
served so sweetly to our senses.
Luckier than the tribe in Namibia
who never had a word for it.

Blue is the color of time,
hydrangeas, herons, crabs, peacocks,
periwinkles, sharks, forget-me-nots,
hearts go blue, too.

Without it, how would one dream
of sailing the ocean to the very
edges of the sky or bask in the
mystery of somewhere else,

—a far-off today to discover your own hue
and the swinging pendulum of living.
Even the darkest shades are capable
of being illuminated by the sun.

PORTRAIT OF PAPA WITH
& WITHOUT HIS COWBOY HAT

Brown bucket top papa's head
with a valley in the center,
mesas round the sides.
Big enough to hide his eyes,
two lonely beetles brimmed
with pain. "*Howdy*," as he tips
the bucket, avoiding eye contact
—his trademark. Does not want
the kids to see in the dirty window,
an old sorrow too long in the sun.
He saddles Pride, his favorite
mustang, then gallops off to Love's
truck stop bar for a drink to wet
his memory. Two eggs, bacon,
sausage, Jim Beam on the rocks.
Under the dim lights, flickering neon,
he takes off his hat and laughs until
the stars sink from another night.

MOTHER ON THE LAWN

She bends dinner spoons into rings
as wind chimes surrender
to the barren wind on a gravel
lawn.

Not a wrinkle upon her face,
        only crow's eyes,
—a Muttley laugh from smoking.
She kicks a rusted ashtray.

Her back curves into the shape
of Delicate Arch, a confidence
eroded by her history. You almost
can't tell; she wears her pain well.

You'd never believe that her mother
committed suicide on her 13th birthday,
leaving her alone to raise her sister,
marked by an absence of youth.

Six shades of blue acrylic
onto plated silver. A few speckles
drip onto the hot concrete. They will
remain, at least until monsoon season.

Then again, that's how it goes;
the world shapes you, then you mold
your own reality. To protect our children,
we bend dinner spoons into rings.

PALO SANTO

On the peak of Camelback Mountain,
I seek healing from a medicine woman.
Her eyes, large wells of whys
that stare deep enough to unravel
the stones of my becoming.
She hands me a bundle of palo santo
to cleanse my home of bad energy.
I ask her if there is a wood
strong enough to erase bad memories.
"No, I am afraid not," she sighs.

Her face transforms into twilight,
and big rain falls as the mountain
slowly erodes into a plateau.

As I prepare to leave, she hands me
an empty glass bottle labeled "Time,"
along with a bill I cannot afford.

YOUR REFLECTION IN MY BECOMING

I see you in the belly of the moon,
a coin-shaped mirror reflecting
all that I am in this moment.

I want to call you via the universe,
toll-free, with my gratitude.

I like the part of me that you represent,
as pure as a spring welling up from the earth.

When I first met you, our fictions
had not yet molded our characters.

My hands were cupped, drinking
the lemonade you squeezed.

I remember singing into your eyes
on balconies above Europe.

We would complain as if the world
owed us a greater gift than being.

In dusked blackberry fields, we'd lay, ignoring
every mosquito to create a worthy picture.

These days I don't count on good graces
or blessings from the sky.

When you get my voicemail, lose this number,
—this is a *rhetorical memorial.*

I am grateful to see myself
clearly through our time together,
a still body of uninterrupted innocence.

SONG INFIDELITY

Singing into the eyes of another
might as well be making love.

Midnight, we howl at our proverbial
moon as we gather in a circle,

cooing,
   plucking,
      barking,
         yelping!

I am the language of music,
where a miscommunication
is only an out-of-key harmony,
wrong chord, or jumbled word,
so easy to forgive.

Melodies like saints,
songs, our confessionals.

So easy to understand
when souls speak.

WATERCOLOR

If I were a paint, I'd be a watercolor.
Indecisive and hard to control,
no one wants to handle watercolors
unless they are brave, patient, or mad.

SEE

How rare to truly see someone,
—not the child playing freely in the fountain,
not the lonely-eyed man in the 64th St. diner window,
not the woman reading a newspaper in the park,
not the refugees in rippling rafts of freedom,
not the Indonesian boy with performing monkeys
barring theater worth more than rupiah,
not the singer playing empty bars across Kansas,
not the seniors playing chess outside the pawnshop,
not the Mexican father crossing the Rio Grande for work,
not the American mother living off tips at the diner,
not the teenager with dreams bigger than ice cream parlors,
not the crowds of millions chanting for equality,
their voices ringing chimes through the world.
How rare to see someone and feel.
How rare to see someone and *know*
you are not alone,
for your eyes are theirs,
your pain, too.
How rare to truly see someone.

SISTERS UNDER THE PINK MOON

Under the pink moon, sisters in arms, chewing dried figs,
sprouts, ginger, chocolates. Tiny kisses on bark, tears
flowing. Always tears but not always the sad kind. Mud
caked like tomorrow on boots. Below skinny-dipping
magnolias in the wintertime, setting intentions upon rogue
leaves in the campfire. May tonight transform us. Come spring,
may we find lily-white flowers pure as a newborn, childhood
dreams without training wheels. May we release the ashes
as we close chapters. May we bloom, may we prosper.
May we embrace the oak of our womanhood. No suitor can
hold a candle to a sister's love. Between our squishy thighs rest
all our secrets, natural beauty, imperfections, painful truths,
feminine magic, loose talk, complexities, understanding,
belonging. Beside Luna's lust figure, we breathe in a smoky
silence as we kindle our uncertainty with a branch.

SAGUARO SKELETON

Scavenging the desert
under the microscope
of the sun, searching for
the skeleton of a saguaro.

Parched on pavement,
we make our way
to Pinnacle Peak
in search of the dead.

The freeze comes
as the elders fall,
as the past begs us
to bring it to life.

DRAWING DESIRE

Every so often, paintings
would arrive from my
incarcerated uncle
—a prisoner in Douglas.
His subjects were often
fallen barns and dead
wheat fields in Wyoming.

As a child, I would draw
lines in desert sands:
big mansions with gardens
full of rosemary, though
no one ever lived there.
They were only structures
to store more desire.

THE GREAT MYSTERY OF PABLO DIABLO

In Idaho, the family dog went missing
as grizzly bears lurked and rivers
growled at each bend, revealing
their white teeth, biting the bedrock.

We yelled his name into the wild,
searching miles beyond our cabin;
far from our shelter of certitude,
we traced each disappearing footstep.

As the palm of the earth released the sun,
our worry grew, the moon a yo-yo
tricking us with every turn,
—our desperation growing.

As the light made a theatrical exit,
I released my prayer into the wind.
"Come home! I have treats,
wool blankets, a face ripe for kissing!"

Still, not a bark. We ceased searching
with grief, reluctantly returning
from the darkness, only to find grandpa
cackling with a jovial pup between his feet.

MONARCH MANTRA #1

Do not spend
all your joy
in one place.
This is only
the beginning.

*(There will be many
places yet.)*

(GOOD VIRTUES)

When she looks out across the Atlantic,
shimmering silver waves of layered horizon,
my sister sees God as a man in flesh
with a mighty hand to cradle and protect.

I watch the water ripple, yet I see
one-thousand possibilities folding over
within the unknown mosaic of time
—humility in the infinite minds of galaxies.

She sees a white man bending down.
I see a tree within a tree, within me.
She sees holy water
where I see a sacred question mark.

The truth is, we both long to arrive
at the celestial table carrying good virtues,
but the vessels in which we arrive
could not be any more different.

MESSENGER

A great horned owl dropped dead

at your feet, New Year's Day 2018, the saddest year of our
young lives—though we didn't know it yet.

We placed the body in a plastic garbage bin,
a creature symbolic of wisdom, left in an irreverent coffin
like a pause after a bad joke.

Months later, in La Luz, New Mexico, you bought me
a Navajo ring made of turquoise, bonded with silver,
but you never found the right time to ask.

Maybe the owl's wings were clipped, or worse,
his soul was parched, searching for the mesquite.
Whatever the destiny, our messenger never delivered.

SMALL SHIPS

Somewhere in London,
bathing in a claw-foot tub
without a voice.

Hot running water
burning my skin,
eucalyptus, clementine.

Ill with a quiet storm
of reeled-in resentment,
you called to ask a favor.

Your words—small ships
crashing on my island.
It was then I knew

I was alone.

THE SILVER LINING OF SUFFERING

Hardships come, bearing gifts
—slow mornings of grasping
love, our only tangible offer,
as the saffron sun pours down pretty,
cutting through clothes hanging on
the line. Or the way grandmother's
quilt drapes gently across a friend's
lap. You never noticed the star-shaped
birthmark under his left ear, but now
it is all you want to see. We are kinder
with tragedy, in a world brazen and
uneasy; for a time, we are calm as
wild horses in an open prairie. With
every small or tremendous hour, open
these presents of fragility and allow
the unraveling ribbon-and-bow moments
to surprise your human condition.
Adapt and reassess, and you will notice
that poppies bloom from cracks in the asphalt.

DEAR DREAMS,

Will you reveal
my path? I am
exhausted.

Sincerely,
Conscious apathy

OLD MONARCH

Standing tall in an Arizona dust storm,
my friend Pablo once said to me
with convincing conviction,
"You are as stable as an old oak."
I was silent, as I often am
when I am offended.

Then *why* do I feel like an old monarch?
    —flying, flying, flying away
only to chase death in the end.
Why do I feel the urgency
of a lonely drop of rain in the Sonoran
escaping the magenta sky?

The yellow paint is chipping
on St. Anthony's favorite cathedral,
the red wine, bitter on my tongue.
A Portuguese singer cries
and I, an old monarch,
will continue on into the unknown
    —flying, flying, flying away
perhaps searching for someone
who sees me as I am.

LONGING
IN FLIGHT

REGARDING NOSTALGIA

Last night, I made my bed in yesterday.
Slept in the languid summer of youth;
us, sticking like two sweet buns between sheets,
the hum of the hypnotic ceiling fan,
unable to break love's spell then and now.

Yesterday is safe to visit, knowing the outcome.
Changing and twisting minor details,
nostalgic craftsmanship, reinstalling my past
to fit my uncertain future,
and abundant denial.

I only choose to see the rose-colored before,
dances under fairy lights, mothers with advice,
smells like evergreen and petunia,
kisses that only lead to gardens of more
mystery, dogs we thought would live forever.

Today is too painful to remain in,
a blur of suitcase cobwebs in messy closets.
So, I lay in yesterday, and I make it sweet,
and when I wake up tomorrow, this will be
a yesterday, too.

BRIDLE PATH (*LONGING IN LYTTELTON*)

As I climb Bridle Path,
a woman twice my age passes me.
She is singing the melody to "Red River Valley,"
as if she is the heroine the cowboy laments.
Desire and longing are the only shoes
you need to climb mountains.
I hope to see you soon.
I've made it to the top.

LUCY

Everyone needs a friend
like Lucy—a beacon of light
as regal as Long Point Lighthouse,
flashing her lily smile in the night,
guiding us sad, lost souls
into her shore.

As reliable as the lizards
around the front door frame
of your childhood home,
except Lucy does not scatter
when you return, she remains
constant as the desert heat.

Everyone needs a friend like Lucy
to build them up, let them cry,
send postcards to, laugh with,
dream bigger than dreams with
when everyone else is too afraid to
let it all in, make it all happen,
let it all be.

HUMAN IMAGINATION

Alone in my bathtub, I am
suddenly struck by an absence

of wonder. When we were children,
friends would say,

"Press your ear up to this seashell,
and you will hear the ocean."

I am now a woman, beginning
to understand the frailty of human

imagination, for when I press the shell
up to my ear, I only hear the running faucet.

IN SMALL MOMENTS

Must it be absence making hearts
grow fonder? Why not the pink
country hue of their lips, kissing
every secret? Or an imperfect dance at
Fran's Dive, knowing every missed step
is only one small misunderstanding?
Why not the silence on short drives
to the grocery store, arguments over
flavors of ice cream and laundry habits,
incomplete sentences, untended gardens,
and intended dreams? The dress might not
always look good, but you say it does every
time. Doesn't that grow a fondness? Unmade
beds, unfinished projects, unread books,
searching for reasons to stay over and over
to finish what you started. Or the way
she cries at the strangest part of the movie,
curling up next to you—a crescent cat
purring for companionship. Why not
apology bouquets or make-up sex or
days spent in hammocks with a list
of to-dos? Why not frozen dinners
in pajamas followed by a spontaneous
splurge on the town, fake accents,
inside jokes, mundane mornings,
clarity walks, burnt coffee, perfect peaches,
cricket-chirping nights, back porch
Woody Guthrie sing-alongs, or holding
hands on the way to the hospital, believing
in the power of love's crutch? Why not
these small moments?

MOSAIC

The last time I saw you,
I broke your mother's china plate
into one-hundred little pieces.

With them, I formed a mosaic
into the shape of your eyes.
But do you still see me the same?

HUMAN TOUCH

I listen to the constant chatter of the universe.
All these sounds keep me company now
—a deluge of foreign languages
passport-ing without palisades.

Do not get me wrong; I respect the laurel,
the cardinal, the humming hound,
but these things are not my dead friend,
standing in the doorway of her red adobe.

Nor my singing sisters round the campfire
harmoniously chanting words of understanding
or my mindful mother quilted in curiosity
 —the fawn cannot tell me I tried my best.

The Redwood Forest is not my lover
running his hand through my hair,
drawing a finger in circles around my breast
as I reply with my own shape.

For these earthly gifts, I am grateful,
but the only thing they cannot do
is throw their arms around me and say,
"I love you, too."

MASTER OF DENIAL (IN THE FORM OF A SONG)

Look! Across the street,
the prettiest houses across from me,
shutters all painted, grass fresh, and cut.

I peer from my side
where all we have, dusty and broken,
pushing the mower to its erosion.

I see the neighbors, their beauty and style,
but I am the master of my own denial.

When the sun is out, it is so easy
to pretend everything is fine and breezy,
—a perfect point of view.

The flowers bloom at the governor's fair
while we breathe in the polluted air
yet, I can only smell their roses.

I can see the earth suffering with every mile,
but I am the master of my own denial.

My mother hides in her bedroom and cries,
trying to break the family ties,
home late from job number two.

The hustle is hard for everyone,
for every mother under the sun.
I never stopped to ask why.

For when her door opened, dinner and a smile,
but I am the master of my own denial.

I peer out west beyond the horizon
and see the plains begin to widen,
imagining a place better than here.

I ran from home, the drab depression,
imagining an escape from the oppression
into the arms of big ideas.

I made leaving some kind of lifestyle
because I am the master of my own denial.

So many towns I see, crumbling in despair,
only the clean ones I boast and share,
—the architecture, the good neighborhoods.

Every place I go, I choose what I see.
I create every good memory
to the point of ill delusion.

In my mind, each sight was filed
because I am the master of my own denial.

Everyone turned a blind eye to bad news
until change and acceptance got confused.
We have become accustomed to the pain.

A world of people who pick and choose
what suits their pockets and their moods
to the detriment of another.

Let's wake up from our guile.
We are the masters of our own denial.

I WAS WRONG

I thought I could make it alone,
but I forgot to pack water.

(Carrying a heavy load in the Sonoran heat.)

One pair of eyes see,
two remember.

(I watched a hummingbird bathe in canyon wash.)

Was it yellow or red?
No one around probing my sight.

(I built the tent and laid my mat across the cold rock.)

No star or owl can lay
a warm hand across my body.

(I woke up to the rain carrying me to the bottom.)

PRISONER OF HER TIME

Here I am
retelling the story

of my grandmother,
who took her own life.

A guinea pig
in the hands of men.

They called her Crazy,
but I will rename her

for what she really was
—a woman born

in the wrong time,
held captive

from great
potential.

A prisoner of
powerful illusions.

YOUNG BLOOD HILL

Ten-mile mule from the Mexican border,
hiking toward a heat in the morning to
visit my friend's ghost. Upon arrival, I lay
in a bouldered armchair befit an emotional
archaeologist, selfishly excavating answers.
Why did I abandon my journey for love?

Swimming through dunes of sand,
sagebrush scraping my knees, eyes
on no prize—a peak is only another
beginning. "Amy, why do I keep returning
to your grave above this town?" My spirit
is hollow, whittled to my essence.

You always suggest I leave to become
a woman our mothers were never allowed
to be. Yet, I am a festering ancestral wound,
a freckle on the elbow of the world, a reticent
roundabout circling around the truth,
begging the dead for therapy.

As I arrive on top, your music echoes through
the boombox canyon. Stumbling up, slow
burn, always afraid. Show me how to be
braver than my grandmothers before me.
Amid the Catholic crosses, candles, flowers:
there you are, setting the sun.

RESILIENCE

Even through death and destruction,
we always find ways to overcome,
crossing the bridge to the other side.

As if never brushing the damage,
we sit in cafés smashing glasses,
forgetting our bad years.

Joan of Arc did not bear her prophecy
with complacency. Only lazy seers
fall to obscurity.

In canopies gracing the sky, a magpie
seeks shiny gifts from the world,
unaware of the vanishing light.

We know the bird would not raze a lifetime
of living over disappearing silver. She will
simply discover another object of desire.

Our minds are malleable as the red clay
our ancestors used to build villages
still standing in this century.

We are more resilient than we know.
I, too, will live through horrible sorrow
and live to tell you in a dimly lit bar, laughing.

THE BEST PART

I have always loved
    beginnings and endings.
Maybe this is my chance
    to embrace the journey.

(Where the story is.)

SHIFTING SANDS

Moments before
the air changes,
we sense an
impending shift.
Though rarely
do we realize
our path when
there is dust
obscuring our
vision.

PRETTY IDEA

You are an impossible kind, haunted
by beauty, a Van Gogh lens of days.
　　　—you cannot be trusted.
Someday, your hunger will become
so ravenous that you will abandon
all other senses to feed your desire.

Ideas—pretty roses, *until*
you prick your thumb. With harvests,
you must also receive my stubborn
will, a New Orleans midnight spur.
Love's genesis is waving from afar,
—seemingly perfect.

In London, you added me to your
gallery wall, another flower. We will
lay together for one-thousand nights,
until you are bloody from holding
my branch, searching for another
pretty idea in the garden.

LAST NIGHT,
I SAW YOU AT THE BAR

Hearing your voice
is like hearing
one-thousand stories
that I have forgotten.

IF I WERE A PAINTER

If I had a box of paints, I would produce hope
from my seat at the celestial table,

—a soft brushstroke stream the color of an Easter egg,
gently rolling along canvas, mornings after rain,

a shy peach tree with blossoms small as dimes
surprising us with fruit in late summer,

red rain boots in sunshine, a hodgepodge of dried mud,
proof we walked through the storm and survived,

a Chinese harbor, whistling fisherman,
net full of silver trout, feast after famine,

a high-speed Irish train, watercolor choir,
"the Auld Triangle, it goes jingle jangle,"

confetti in the streets, splatter of peace,
a parade of pedestrians ringing and free,

the crow, the robin, the fox, the deer,
I would paint a portrait of each.

I would create an escape
with every drywall embrace.

If I were a painter,
if I had a box of paints.

SAYING GOODBYE

At home, lighting candles for the dead.
In this sacred place, I lie, dreaming
of cottonwood trees and lazy days
under heartache's weeping willow.
I burn the toast every single time,
read my favorite authors much too fast.
Perhaps there is an answer in every ending,
but what I truly want is to get better at saying
goodbye. Hold the gaze, make amends.
Let the heavy blanket of grief press down
on me, with a knowing I can always
get out of bed, draw the curtains back,
wash every dish until I forget.
Light another candle for yesterday,
one for tomorrow, too, and one for
every fleeting moment in-between.
I want to get the toast right this time.
I want to be better at saying goodbye.

SEWING INSTRUCTIONS

I still long to apologize
—to the animal whisperer; a prideful
old barn woman full of baby chicks
and pups, her wire hair curling into frame,
kind, mean, complicated. Aren't we all?

She might have been your bartender
once, serving stiff small-town medicine,
eight-ball fights, galloping gossip, news,
karaoke, blues, you could borrow her light,
and never return it.

In Portugal I wrote her a letter outside
the Sé de Lisboa, hoping strangers begging
for mercy might spare me some
when a stolen backpack became my censor
        —a gateway to more silence.

So, I returned home and began to sew
with an old Singer machine her son bought me
years prior. Blue string for integrity, pink squares
for unconditional love. Is it enough to be
warm with intention?

REASONS

You loved me
when I was empty
until I needed you
in unhealthy ways.
This is why I must
get my fill alone.

A FATE I HAVE CHOSEN

At times, I punish myself
by reaching out to you
in the middle of the day.

Hands so empty they
could disappear, a rabbit
in heartbreak's magic hat.

I was softer beside you,
pliant as paint. Now
sentient and shapeless.

Our ending— a hurricane,
sidewalks flooding
as I built a raft.

Yellow lanterns,
an oily blur. With time,
I am indistinct.

You reply with kindness,
a fate
even worse than spite.

POINT OF VIEW

Hearts are transporting
dangerous goods.
Anxious, while wading
through the unknown forest,
searching for lost treasure
      —a part of me
only lovers can reveal.
The problem is, I see
the Nantucket sunset *once*
and believe it's forever.

MONARCH MANTRA #2

Come to peace
with yourself
before it is
too late.

(There is still time.)

A YEAR OF VALENTINE'S DAYS

A bloated red moon floats over Sedona.
The universe is handing me a rose.
It knows I am lonely. The great sky
never delivers what you expect,
only surprises shrouded in bundles
of more questions, beckoning us to desire
what we cannot have, propelling us,
bestowing perfect hearts with painful endings
—a good night for every well-lived day.
Standing below Cathedral Rock, the beauty
too much to bear. For a moment, I deny
our inevitable impermanence while
graciously receiving the flower. Good night.

THE BRIDGE

You, too, can choose
to cross

or you can stay
on the other side

where you are safe
in the past,

but you should know,
once you do,

you are free to
infinite arrivals

—a lifetime of chances
come from taking the first step.

THE HOUSES WE BUILD

I am here to tell you
that I have accepted good things.
I remember being a cynic once.
Denying myself the sip of holy wine
while the birds were singing in their nests,
I waited for the world to end.
Mindlessly, I accepted the dances,
the roses, pink moons, and the sacred "now."
We can so easily turn every joyous thing
into some perilous warning sign.
Our pasts are cruel carpenters,
hammering away,
building walls around our hearts,
until every corner is cluttered
with cobwebs and childhood trauma.
I am here to tell you I grabbed the broom,
the rusted old shovel, and did the work.
I no longer wait for lovers to leave
or for the earth to rattle beneath me.
I am here to tell you
what a relief it is.

EUCALYPTUS TREE

(My Arrival to Rest)

ABSENCE OF ALWAYS

Aren't we all searching for permanence
in our gods, friendships, and partners?
Knowing our flesh may someday rot,
dodging death with human delicacy
—our vows like glass.

We try to carry love letters from closets,
language on stone, some remanence
of stored nostalgia, names carved, praying
to a maple tree by simply unknowing its end,
pictures framed, warranties promising "built to last."

Our eyes meet the seemingly endless Lake Huron.
We stare for hours simply because we cannot
see the other side, though each season is reliable
as the last. We are always seeking forevers
to try to fill our beautiful impermanence.

MORNING MEDITATION

Running in my mind toward a meadow,
through acres of rippled marsh, pooled boots, soiled knees.
Long past childhood, mother's tears behind doorframes,
her bad taste in bad men, past the schoolyard girls who
taunted my joy of singing—confidence thieves.

Past the dead mesquite where I'd wait for my father,
stumbling around his absence, the beech barn falling
from the flood, no heart for hammer in sight. Beyond
the fence line, a sunset is freed from every horizon,
promising hopeful years ahead.

Panting past the awkward dance of adolescent love, then you,
true blue. Thirsty now, heart rate's up as I yearn for your touch.
Hands reaching, a co-dependent leech, I need you. I need you,
so I know I am alive. I pause to catch my breath and linger in our
time together, sprawling millions of miles—a whole decade of us.

You better believe love gets two stanzas. Past your infidelity,
heartbreak, anorexia, apple trees, dirty laundry, the darkest
nights birth dawn hatching as I catch my reflection in a pond,
and finally accept my crooked teeth. My boots are soaked,
elbows scraped, hard to believe there was ever an *us* at all.

Trudging ahead, running, running, running! Past it all, and
all we name trauma. Past the broken-down RV, addictions,
concussions, grief, out-of-tune pianos, old dogs dying,
chickens eating crops, family spiraling into madness.
Yes, can't you see I must run somewhere simple?

I am slowing toward the meadow, where there is nothing
but monarchs on milkweed, a rising river flowing toward
a land of afters. I will lay my tired body down in gracious
grasses of gratitude. Once I arrive at the meadow in my
mind, I can make it another day on earth.

OLD DREAMS

Once, I wanted it all.

Love, a white picket fence:
my fantasies, beggars in mercy's
alley. Yet, I felt strangled
by the pressure. Fear is ivy
in a garden of future failures,
swallowing my harvest.

No, I didn't want to end up
like poor old Sisyphus,
fated to push that
goddamn boulder
up that goddamn hill
for eternity. The view
is always the same.
You start to predict
what happens next.

So, I gave it all up
for a chance at freedom,
watched old dreams
roll down the hill,
sat for a while,
and enjoyed the view
from the bottom.

A REMINDER OF JOYFUL SOUNDS:
(CURE FOR APATHY)

- wholehearted laughter
- one single note on a grand piano in a barn
- friends quietly humming along to music
  thinking no one can hear them
- absolute silence
- wind through trees
- choirs on cold streets
- bikes on cobblestone in Amsterdam
- noises old houses make
- bonfires crackling in dry air
- the tone of a mother's comfort
- a dog happily panting
- unexpected summer storms, windows wide open
- the soft, tired voice of a loved one when
  they start falling asleep while talking

NANTUCKET MIDNIGHT STORM

A terrible storm rolled through
in the middle of summer's epilogue.
Every window, open as an empty jar,
my body limp, soaking its weight,
eyes wide, I waited for the page-turner
of seasons. Behind the wrath of wind
and rain, old patient Luna waited
as one often does in times of turmoil.
What will become of the world
when the worst part passes?
What will this night take from us?
Who will emerge from the wreckage
and live to tell the tale?

ONCE IN A LIFETIME

There is a one-in-four-trillion chance
that you exist at all.
If you have any love letters—send them *now*.

MEMORY OF CONTENTMENT

When the fog reclines in the hills of Half Moon Bay,
I am transported back in time to a specific November.
An autumn drive on a frosty footnote, a memory that
invades my senses—a soul-souvenir.

> *Chain-smoking American Spirits out your car*
> *window as I froze in the passenger seat*
> *   —brisk breeze planting rosy cheeks.*
> *Our silence, a marigold monogamy. Our*
> *love, still thick as the air. It was a day*
> *like many, not happy or sad, passing small-*
> *town grocers and crosswalks, believing I could*
> *live forever in one moment—a pure memory*
> *of contentment to which I never cease returning.*

ABANDONED LOVE

If I were to leave this world tomorrow,
let it be known I loved you only.

A cavern in my being carries a lucky coin,
a melody ghost, your piercing spell.

Long years I've spent chasing my own tail,
running to distract the inevitable pause.

May you know in the end
why I chose to be alone.

Open-hearted orphan, your Annie,
bound to cycles of absent fathers.

You tried to break my habit,
and I went spinning, your addict.

Tonopah, rolling in the bed of a pickup
down a gravel road, your tender trace.

On a red dirt ranch riding a mule,
your natural-born escape artist.

I waited for you to show, and when you
didn't, I rode forever until the stars appeared.

MODERN NOSTRADAMUS

They will speak long after
it is too late. When the fireworks
have faded from your eyes,
you will sit piss drunk,
slurring complaints
on an oaky piano bench
in the middle of a hurricane.
Your mother will say, "*Honey*,
he was wrong all along,"
as if she is some modern
Nostradamus, claiming
visions of love's impending
doom. Isn't it funny how
everyone knows once
the pain sets in? Like
in the middle of a storm,
when your brother shouts,
"I told you we should have
bought a generator!"

EVERY VERSION OF YOU

I wish I had said,
"I love who you will become."
    —a selfish act embalmed,
        to ask you to remain captive
        of our before.

SAILING

To see Bainbridge fading to a sliver,
washed ashore the maple sky
like a memory you can't grasp,
yet you always try.

The earworm of "I'll Be Seeing You."
We always remember the places
we can never return to but wish for
with all we are.

I have been leaving since day one.
My mother sent me off on the raft
of human eternity, sailing into
nuances of consciousness.

Through the years, I redraw the map
back to these childhood illusions.
An invisible intuition, my compass.
Curiosity, my detrimental North Star.

The sun is fading into pink and purple
like a bruise discovered after an evening
of drinking. Its arrival perplexing, a
propeller ready to sink at any moment.

My existence floats into view
as the boat docks.
How marvelous to see land
reflected in an ocean of uncertainty.

MONARCH MANTRA #3

When you learn
nature's secrets,
you will practice
more humanity.

(You will arrive at yourself.)

A PORTRAIT OF MADELINE
AS A WOMAN

She is an old woman
wise beyond her years, stubborn
with dogma.

Age doesn't matter when you are
the man of your own
temple.

Lovers linger in her doorway
but are never courageous
enough to meet her inside.

By the salt river some years
back, a wicker basket landed
on her cottonwood shore,

filled to the brim with sacred
thorn apple, poisonous when
consumed raw.

She lit bundles on fire and sang,
then spent her remainder of days
in a rustic blue adobe,

filled with paints, pecans,
Navajo silver. She rocks back
and forth, chairing time,

too sure for men and their construct
of freedom: proving womanhood can
belong to days.

THE WHERE

Where hardly matters.

Though, I do remember a snowstorm,

blackberries still ripe on sad sage vines,

a golden retriever gnawing on wool,

a sobriety, an unexpected stillness,

wheels on ice, carrying our baggage,

spinning out of control, internally,

figuratively and physically rolling from you.

You, who accepted all my strangeness.

Don't you know I am a desert girl?

Never been cold a day in my life.

Mystery is why we hang around.

I suppose that is why I left

—no chains or salted highways.

When we lose ourselves,

we leave to remember.

HOW TO GRIEVE

In late hours of my hotel room,
I converse with my shadow,
its body fuller than mine
on a bed made of feathers
from geese that once bathed
in a pond in China.

We can witness the end of others,
but we will never know
the end of ourselves.
Parmenides said *motion*
does not exist, but I am always
escaping

—away from lonely beginnings,
as they present no end.
I am here to prove Parmenides
wrong. Love and death are inevitable,
and at the end of each, I am *moving.*

DANCING DREAM

Last night I became an old mansion,
ornamented with dances in haunted rooms.

Waltzing across kitchens bigger than
my one-bedroom apartment.

Échappé outside to the garden,
toward a bush shaped like a crying swan.

Faceless strangers filled every hazed space,
but my subconsciousness floated toward my ex.

The dance continued until I became
a lonely merry-go-round circling togetherness.

GHOST IN TOWN

1. Hello, I am your ghost in town.
   Ding-dong, here to haunt you,
   even while summer lilacs bend,
   revealing infant views between
   wild oaks, older but still alive.

2. You changed the locks:
   a key to a new life
   without me, fresh start,
   clean slate.

3. I have come to show you, my spirit is a beggar.
   My plan is to get in touch without speaking,
   knock my favorite mug off your wicker shelf,
   dance in your doorway to create a shiver.

4. *These actions tell,*
   please don't forget me.

5. I have become invisible matter
   who no longer matters to you.
   Hollow as an empty grave,
   frightening you with my
   memory.
   (I want to scare you into my realm.)

6. Definition of ghost:
   a disembodied soul

7. You are packing my belongings and moving away.

   Underwear, socks, tchotchkes, jewelry, diaries, jackets,
   linens, candles, photographs.

   I am still here.

IF YOU ARE LUCKY

If you are lucky, you will get to see the sunrise
over the Atlantic as a pin drops in the quiet
of a waking world.

Hands will hold yours for longer than a minute,
maybe long enough to call it love,
stretching over years.

You will witness wild wings of a hummingbird,
suckling sweet tea from a red feeder, as
grandma watches from her kitchen window

—afternoon light illuminating her gray eyes.
If you're lucky, you will always remember
that moment, sweet as nectar.

You will grow old enough to accept your own
depressed humility and bask in the glory
of imperfection.

To be flawed is to be the deepest, most human
part of yourself. If you are lucky, you will look
in the mirror one day and see someone you like.

The storm will roll in, rumbling in time
as you sing in harmonious blossoms
of friendship.

You will stay up until a dealing dawn
holding your stomach, swallowing a belly
of laughter on Tennessee's porch.

If you're lucky, someone will break your heart,
and you will truly understand
the circle of life

—you will cry until you see the world
from a different point of view, soft with
the vulnerability of experience.

You will grieve one-million selves and
transform, as life's rocking chair
surprises you with a constant back and forth.

If you're lucky, you will have a walk
ruined by the rain, but only if you are
truly lucky, will you embrace it.

You will kiss the foreheads of
your children and raise them
to be lucky, too.

If you're lucky, tomorrow will come,
and it might not be quite like yesterday,
but the arrival is what matters.

AGAINST ALL ODDS

Let this nightmare make you softer, watching every new
leaf turn us into spring. Cardinals of hope, born in nests
ever-changing. The first tulip. The color yellow never felt
so important. Let it reveal the blue skies, cherry blossoms,
and smells of your neighbor's cooking. Let it inspire you
to call a friend and say, I am sorry. I love you. I cherish you.
Our sweet memories are a museum in which I have
a lifelong admission. Let it break down every petty
fear of loving, make you compassionate for strangers,
their anonymous suffering, and come to reckon with
your own suffering. Listen to Nina Simone or free
jazz. Listen to those who created against all odds. Or,
with each quiet hour, sew your thoughts in fertile ground
so they may blossom.

Please, let this nightmare make you softer.

WAKING UP TO LIVE

When you start to grow old,
apathy might burrow in you.

Naked on a coastal crest,
screaming at the end of the earth.

You must go mad
to remind yourself of being:

Jump on motel beds,
join a drunken choir,
two-step with a stranger,
drive through the night
for a serendipitous meeting,
make yourself a fool, and
wade through the darkness
to reach Orion's Belt.

From these places,
you can relearn how to live;
otherwise, you might already be
gone.

SOME TOMORROW

Some tomorrow
when I am gone,
bury me in a garden.
Indian paintbrush,
lilac, and lavender.
Yellow raincoat tulips
all shaded by
a maple perhaps,
or a weeping willow.
Whatever roots
care enough
to grow strong,
bury me among them.
I want to become
every seed of possibility
I could not plant
while I was alive.

With longing,
  Courtney Marie

INDEX

Andrews McMeel Publishing
a division of Andrews McMeel Universal
1130 Walnut Street, Kansas City, Missouri 64106

www.andrewsmcmeel.com

Illustrations by Daren Thomas Magee

21 22 23 24 25 BVG 10 9 8 7 6 5 4 3 2 1

ISBN: 978-1-5248-6562-7

Library of Congress Control Number: 2020949269

Editor: Patty Rice
Art Director/Designer: Julie Barnes
Production Editor: Jasmine Lim
Production Manager: Carol Coe

ATTENTION: SCHOOLS AND BUSINESSES
Andrews McMeel books are available at quantity discounts with bulk purchase for educational, business, or sales promotional use. For information, please e-mail the Andrews McMeel Publishing Special Sales Department: specialsales@amuniversal.com.